TALES OF INVENTION

The
COMPUTER

Chris Oxlade

Heinemann Library

Chicago, Illinois

www.heinemannraintree.com
Visit our website to find out
more information about
Heinemann-Raintree books.

To order:
☎ Phone 888-454-2279
💻 Visit www.heinemannraintree.com
to browse our catalog and order online.

Edited by Louise Galpine and Laura Knowles
Designed by Philippa Jenkins
Original illustrations © Capstone Global Library Ltd 2011
Illustrated by KJA-artists.com
Picture research by Mica Brancic
Originated by Capstone Global Library Ltd
Printed and bound in China by CTPS

15 14 13 12 11
10 9 8 7 6 5 4 3 2 1

Library of Congress Cataloging-in-Publication Data
Oxlade, Chris.
  The computer / Chris Oxlade.
      p. cm. -- (Tales of invention)
  Includes bibliographical references and index.
  ISBN 978-1-4329-3829-1 (hc) -- ISBN 978-1-4329-3836-9
(pb) 1. Computers--Juvenile literature. I. Oxlade, Chris
II. Title.
  QA76.23.093 2011
  004--dc22
                                        2009049147

Acknowledgments
The author and publisher are grateful to the following
for permission to reproduce copyright material: Alamy
pp. **10** (© Interfoto), **11** (© United Archives GmbH), **14**
(© Interfoto), **17** (© Peter Jordan), **22** (© Interfoto), **27**
(© Stock Connection); Corbis pp. **5** (dpa Corbis/© A3250
Oliver Ber), **15** (Science Faction/© Michael Rosenfeld),
16 (ClassicStock/© D&P Valenti), **19** (© Haruyoshi
Yamaguchi), **21** (© Andrew Brusso); Getty Images pp. **6**
(Science & Society Picture Library), **8** (Science & Society
Picture Library), **9** (Science & Society Picture Library),
13 (Time & Life Pictures), **18**, **23** (Peter Macdiarmid);
Photolibrary pp. **4** (Imagebroker.net/Kreutzer Kreutzer),
7 (Imagestate/The Print Collector), **12** (Imagestate/The
National Archives), **25** (Mauritius), **26** (Stockbroker/
Monkey Business Images Ltd); Shutterstock p. **24**
(Monkey Business Images).

Cover photographs of a laptop computer reproduced
with permission of Reuters/© Jorge Silva and a man
using a calculating machine invented by M. Thomas
DeColmar in around 1820 reproduced with permission
of Corbis/© Bettmann.

We would like to thank Ian Graham for his invaluable
help in the preparation of this book.

Every effort has been made to contact copyright holders
of material reproduced in this book. Any omissions will
be rectified in subsequent printings if notice is given to
the publisher.

All the Internet addresses (URLs) given in this book
were valid at the time of going to press. However, due
to the dynamic nature of the Internet, some addresses
may have changed, or sites may have changed or
ceased to exist since publication. While the author
and publisher regret any inconvenience this may cause
readers, no responsibility for any such changes can be
accepted by either the author or the publisher.

CONTENTS

Look for these boxes

Biographies

These boxes tell you about the life of inventors, the dates when they lived, and their important discoveries.

Setbacks

Here we tell you about the experiments that didn't work, the failures, and the accidents.

EUREKA!

These boxes are about important events and discoveries, and what inspired them.

Any words appearing in the text in bold, **like this**, are explained in the glossary.

TIMELINE

2010—The timeline shows you when important discoveries and inventions were made.

COMPUTERS IN OUR LIVES

This book is about the invention of computers. But what exactly is a computer? Put simply, a computer is a machine that follows a list of instructions called a **program**. By changing the program we can make it do all sorts of jobs for us. For example, a personal computer is used to play games, display photographs, write text, or play music—just by changing its program.

Computers are everywhere in our modern lives. There are millions of computers in offices, storing all sorts of information about products and customers. At home, we use them to send emails, browse the **Internet**, communicate with friends, play games, watch movies, and do many other jobs.

When you use a computer, do you ever wonder how it was invented?

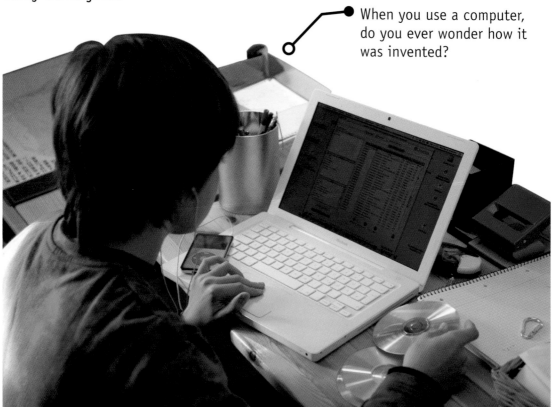

around 3000 BCE
—The abacus
is invented in
Mesopotamia

This supercomputer, known as Jugene, is one of the fastest computers in the world. It is used by scientists at a German research center.

Scientists use powerful computers called supercomputers for jobs such as weather forecasting. There are also many computers that we never see because they are hidden away inside other machines. These "embedded" computers are found in cars, MP3 players, phones, digital cameras, and medical equipment such as X-ray scanners.

EUREKA!

Early computers were extremely big and expensive, and were only used by scientists and large businesses. In 1975 the first personal computer was invented. Since then the number of personal computers has grown quickly. Today, there are more than a billion—that's one for every six people in the world. Every year, the number of personal computers goes up by 7.5 percent.

around 200 BCE
—The ancient Chinese begin using the abacus

BEFORE COMPUTERS

The story of computers begins with mechanical calculating machines. The oldest mechanical calculator is the abacus. An abacus is made up of beads on wires or in grooves. Each bead represents the number 1, 5, or 10. Adding and subtracting is done by moving beads from side to side. The abacus was probably invented more than 5,000 years ago by people of an ancient civilization called Mesopotamia. It was also used in ancient China, and it is still used in some parts of the world today.

In about 1642, French mathematician Blaise Pascal invented the first automatic adding machine. It used a system of gear wheels to add two numbers together.

Pascal's mechanical calculator could count up to 10 million. Only a few of Pascal's machines survive today.

1642—Blaise Pascal invents a calculating machine

Blaise Pascal (1623–1662)

French mathematician and scientist Blaise Pascal was a brilliant child who wrote books on mathematics when he was only 16. At the age of 19, he built a mechanical adding machine to help his father, who was a tax official, speed up his calculations. Pascal built several machines but sold only a few because the machines were extremely expensive. He died at just 39 years old.

Programmed machines

The idea of programming was thought of long before computers were invented. A common example is the loom. A loom is a machine that weaves cloth. Looms called Jacquard looms had sets of cards with holes in them. Each set of cards was a **program** that made the loom weave a different pattern in the cloth. The invention of the Jacquard loom made weaving complicated patterns easier, faster, and cheaper.

The programming cards can be seen at the top of the Jacquard loom in this illustration.

Babbage's Engines

In the early 1800s, Englishman Charles Babbage got fed up with finding mistakes in tables of numbers in his mathematics books. He decided to build a mechanical calculating machine that could do the complicated sums needed to print the tables accurately. After 10 years of hard work, he had a design for an amazingly complicated machine crammed full of cogs and levers. It was called the Difference Engine. However, Babbage never completed it. Instead he began to invent a new, even more complicated machine. He called this his Analytical Engine.

Babbage never built his Analytical Engine, either, but his designs show what the machine would have been like. The design featured a section that did calculations, a **memory** section for storing results, an input section where numbers were entered, and an output section where results were printed. Babbage planned to use cards with different patterns of holes in them to control the machine. The Analytical Engine would have been similar to a modern computer, but in mechanical form.

In 1991 a team of engineers at London's Science Museum built this Difference Engine using Babbage's plans.

1801—Joseph Marie Jacquard invents the programmable loom

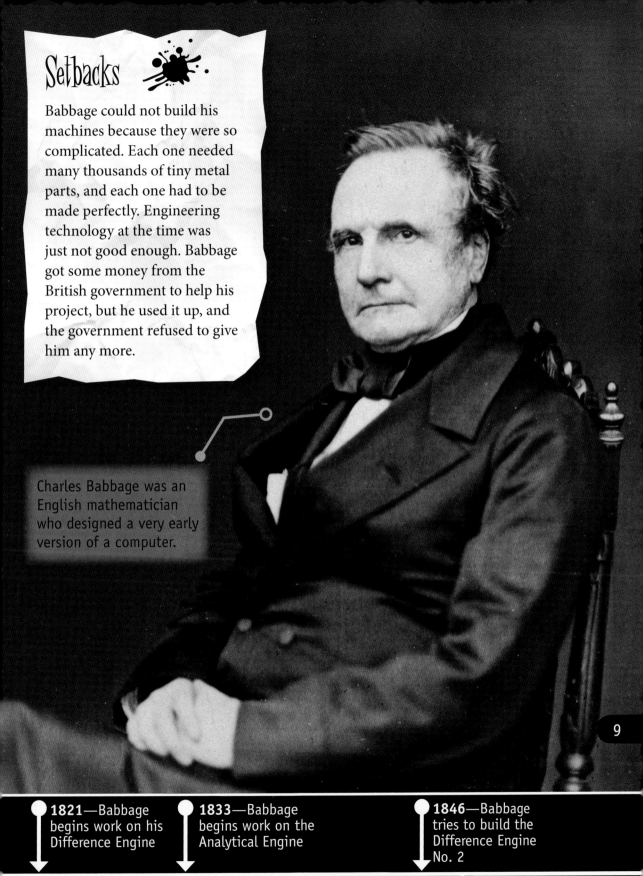

Setbacks

Babbage could not build his machines because they were so complicated. Each one needed many thousands of tiny metal parts, and each one had to be made perfectly. Engineering technology at the time was just not good enough. Babbage got some money from the British government to help his project, but he used it up, and the government refused to give him any more.

Charles Babbage was an English mathematician who designed a very early version of a computer.

1821—Babbage begins work on his Difference Engine

1833—Babbage begins work on the Analytical Engine

1846—Babbage tries to build the Difference Engine No. 2

1850

ELECTRIC COMPUTERS

All modern computers are electric machines. Tiny electric **currents** in their electric circuits control them and represent numbers. The development of electric computers began in the 1930s with the invention of **electromechanical** computers—computers with some electrical parts and some mechanical parts. They used electromagnetic switches called relays to control the flow of electricity. These computers were big enough to fill a room, but less powerful than modern-day pocket calculators. The very first electromechanical computer, the Z1, was built in Germany in 1938 by Konrad Zuse.

By 1941 Zuse had built his third machine, the Z3, despite working full-time as an aircraft engineer during World War II. The Z3 was the first programmable computer.

Konrad Zuse *(1910–1995)*

Konrad Zuse built his computers in a workshop in Berlin, Germany. He wanted a machine that could do complicated engineering calculations. Most of the parts came from old telephone equipment. The workshop was destroyed in World War II, during an air raid on the city. The Z3 machine was lost, but Zuse had already escaped with its successor, the Z4. Zuse's work remained unknown outside Germany until after the end of the war. Later in his life, Zuse designed the world's first computer **program** to play chess.

EUREKA!

Zuse realized that the best way to represent numbers inside a computer is in binary form. Binary uses only zeros and ones, which are easy to represent by turning an electric current on or off. All modern computers use binary.

11

1936—Alan Turing describes a modern-day computer

1938—Konrad Zuse builds the first electromechanical computer

Code-breaking Colossus

In Great Britain in 1943, work was completed on a computer called Colossus. It contained 1,500 **vacuum tubes** that worked as electronic switches. Colossus was designed to break top-secret German codes during World War II (1939–45). Intercepted German radio messages were fed into Colossus, which tried to match letters in the messages with letters produced by equations. When a match was found, the messages could be decoded. The Germans never found out that Colossus was breaking their codes, and the computer remained top secret for decades after the war ended.

This is the Colossus Mark II computer. Messages that it had decoded showed that the Germans had fallen for an Allied trick just before **D-Day**.

1940— Turing builds the Bombe to decipher German codes

1941— Zuse completes his Z3 machine

1943—The Battle of the Atlantic is won against German submarines

1943— The Colossus computer is completed

1944—The Allies land in France on D-Day

1944—Engineers at Harvard and **IBM** build the Harvard Mark 1

Alan Turing (1912–1954)

In 1936 English mathematician Alan Turing wrote about a machine that he imagined in his head. It had a processing unit, **memory**, and a **program** to control it. These are all features of modern computers. During World War II, Turing designed an **electromechanical** computer called the Bombe that helped to break codes produced by Germany's Enigma coding machines. Messages decoded by the Bombe helped the **Allies** to track the movements of German submarines. Turing also worked on the Colossus computer. After the war, Turing designed electronic computers. Turing was a pioneer of **artificial intelligence**. He wrote down the Turing Test. A computer would pass the test if a person asked the same questions of the computer and a human, but could not tell which was which from the answers. So far no computer has passed the Turing Test.

13

045
Zuse's Z3
destroyed
an air
d

1946—ENIAC
is the first
fully electronic
computer

1947—Bell
Laboratories
announces the
transistor

1950

Advances in electronics

In the mid-1940s, fully electronic computers such as the ENIAC were developed. Their **vacuum tubes** were more reliable and hundreds of times faster than the mechanical switches in **electromechanical** computers. However, there were problems with these vacuum tubes, too. They used up a lot of electricity, they gave out a lot of heat, they often had problems, and they took up a lot of space.

Transistors

A group of scientists at the Bell Laboratories in New Jersey began trying to invent a replacement for the vacuum tube. The leader of the group at the Bell Laboratories was a physicist named William Shockley. Two senior members were Walter Brattain and John Bardeen. They experimented with a type of material called a **semiconductor** and eventually made the first **transistor** in 1947. It was much smaller and more reliable than a vacuum tube.

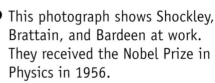

This photograph shows Shockley, Brattain, and Bardeen at work. They received the Nobel Prize in Physics in 1956.

Transistor battle

The invention of the transistor did not run smoothly. The leader, Shockley, worked mainly from home. He became angry when Brattain and Bardeen made an important breakthrough at the laboratory without telling him. Shockley then worked on his own and eventually built a transistor himself.

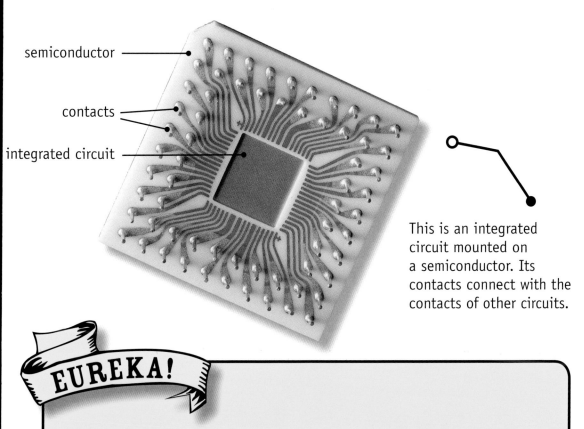

semiconductor

contacts

integrated circuit

This is an integrated circuit mounted on a semiconductor. Its contacts connect with the contacts of other circuits.

EUREKA!

The **integrated circuit** was invented by Jack Kilby at the TI company in 1958. An integrated circuit, also called a **microchip**, is a complete electronic circuit built on a single piece of silicon (a semiconductor). A single integrated circuit can contain millions of transistors, **resistors**, and **capacitors**. Integrated circuits are very small and do not cost a lot to make. Today, they are used in nearly all electrical goods, not just computers.

1958—The integrated circuit (microchip) is invented

1960

THE PERSONAL COMPUTER

In the early 1970s, the world of computers was changed by the invention of the **microprocessor**. A microprocessor contains all the important parts of a computer on a single **microchip**. The very first microprocessor was the Intel 4004. The microprocessor made it possible to build a small, cheap computer, and so the personal computer was invented. The first personal computer was the Altair, built in 1975. It was soon followed by the first Apple computer, the Apple I, invented by Steve Wozniak.

In the late 1970s, computers were invented for people to use at home. These "home" computers were quite cheap. Some came in kits that people had to put together. Most home computers were large keyboards with all the working parts inside. They were normally plugged into a television set.

The Radio Shack TRS-80 shown in this photograph was one of the first home computers.

The IBM PC

International Business Machines (**IBM**) realized that companies could use personal computers for office tasks. In 1981 it developed its own personal computer, the IBM PC. Other manufacturers copied the IBM PC, making "IBM compatibles" that could use **programs** designed for the IBM PC.

Sir Clive Sinclair

(born 1940)

Sir Clive Sinclair is a British inventor and businessman. He learned about electronics while he was in school, and he went on to invent many electronic gadgets. In 1972 his company designed and sold one of the first pocket calculators. In the early 1980s, Sinclair designed home computers, including the Timex Sinclair Spectrum 1000 and the Timex Sinclair 2068. Millions of people learned how to program a computer on Sinclair's machines.

1969—The first two computers on the **Internet** are linked

1970—The computer mouse receives a **patent**

Software

Computers are made up of two parts—**hardware** and **software**. By changing a computer's software, we can change the job it does. On a personal computer there are two types of software—system software and **application** software. System software controls all the parts of the computer and allows users to do jobs such as deleting or moving **files**. **MS-DOS** was one of the first types of system software for personal computers. Applications are pieces of software that make the computer do different jobs. Examples of applications are word processors, games, web-design **programs**, and email programs.

This early version of the computer mouse looks very different from those we use today.

EUREKA!

The computer mouse was invented in the late 1960s by U.S. computer scientist Douglas Engelbart. This was long before there were any personal computers. Engelbart never got any money for his invention, and at the time he had no idea that one day every desktop computer would have a mouse!

1971—Intel releases the Intel 4004 computer

1972—Clive Sinclair sells the first pocket calculators

1972—The first home video-game consoles are introduced. The computer game Pong is released.

1975—Altair is the first personal computer

1975—Bill Gates and Paul Allen start a company called Microsoft

Bill Gates *(born 1955)*

In 1975, at the young age of 19, Bill Gates founded Microsoft with his business partner, Paul Allen. It is now the world's biggest software company. Microsoft software is used on nearly all computers, and Gates has become one of the richest people on the planet. Microsoft's first success came from MS-DOS, a program that Gates wrote himself. Gates now works mainly for his charity foundation, which aims to reduce poverty and improve health around the world.

19

1978—Space
Invaders game
is released

THE INTERNET

The **Internet** was never really invented. It began in 1969 when the U.S. government's Advanced Research Projects Agency (ARPA) linked together computers at different science research laboratories in California. More computers were added, and the **network** became known as ARPANET. During the 1970s, other networks around the world were linked to ARPANET. Scientists used ARPANET to share information and exchange messages, which became known as emails.

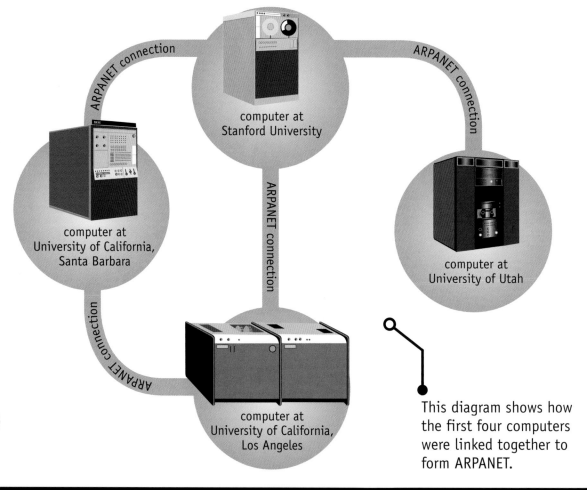

ARPANET connection

computer at Stanford University

ARPANET connection

computer at University of California, Santa Barbara

ARPANET connection

computer at University of Utah

ARPANET connection

computer at University of California, Los Angeles

This diagram shows how the first four computers were linked together to form ARPANET.

1981—Sinclair introduces the Timex Sinclair Spectrum 1000

1981—**IBM** releases its IBM personal computer. **MS-DOS** is released on the IBM PC.

1985—First version of Microsoft Windows is released

In 1980 English **software** consultant Tim Berners-Lee wrote a **program** for storing and linking **files** together on his computer. In 1989 Berners-Lee extended the idea to link files on one computer to files on any other computer on a network. He wrote a coding system called HTML, which allowed people to put links in their files. He also made software for accessing the files across the Internet, and a program called a browser to display the HTML files. The collection of linked information was called the World Wide Web. It was launched in 1991.

Social networks

A social network is a group of people who belong to a sort of online club. They exchange messages and photographs over the Internet. There are lots of these networks, both general and more specialized. The most popular social network websites are MySpace, Facebook, and Twitter.

Tim Berners-Lee launched the World Wide Web in 1991. By 2008 there were more than one trillion web pages on the Internet.

1989—Tim Berners-Lee invents web browsing and the World Wide Web

COMPUTER ENTERTAINMENT

The very first computer game was a simple bat-and-ball game called Pong, which appeared in arcades in 1972. A similar game appeared on the very first video-game console, the Magnavox Odyssey, released in the same year. A video-game console is a computer that is designed specially for playing games. Since the 1970s, consoles have become more and more powerful, and games have become amazingly complicated.

Some classic games include Space Invaders (1978), Pac Man (1980), Donkey Kong (1981), Tetris (1985), and Super Mario Bros (1985). Games can also be played on personal computers. Games were popular on the home computers of the early 1980s, such as the Timex Sinclair 2068. In the middle of the 1990s, personal computers became powerful enough for game playing, too.

This 1970s family plays *Pong* on a video-game console.

1991—The World Wide Web starts working

1993—The **MP3 file** format is introduced

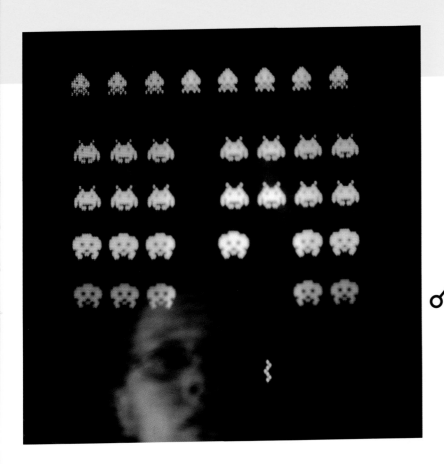

The game Space Invaders helped to make computer games the success they are today.

Space Invaders

Space Invaders was released in 1978. It was designed by Tomohiro Nishikado of Japan. Nishikado decided that the player should shoot aliens because he did not like the idea of shooting at people, even in a game. In Japan, the arcade game was so popular that it caused a shortage of the coins needed to operate the arcade machines.

EUREKA!

Today, online multiplayer games allow players anywhere in the world to play and compete against each other. The most popular of these games is World of Warcraft. It has more than 11 million players.

23

1998—The first MP3 players are released

2000

Music and video

MP3 files were developed at the Fraunhofer Institute in Germany in the late 1980s and early 1990s. One of the leading computer scientists involved was Karlheinz Brandenburg, an expert in math and electronics. The idea of MP3 was to compress music **files** so that they took up much less space in a computer's **memory**.

The job of an MP3 player is to turn MP3 files into sounds. The player has a memory where the files are stored. It takes information from the file and uses it to make an electrical signal that it sends to headphones. The first MP3 players appeared in 1998.

MP3 players are very popular today. Many people use them to listen to music or watch videos while they are on the move.

24

2001—Apple introduces its first iPod

2004—Facebook social networking is launched

2005—Microsoft releases its Xbox 360 console

2000

2005

Sharing music

Music and video files are easy to copy from one computer to another. People often share music and video files with their friends. However, these files are normally copyrighted, which means by law you are not allowed to share them with other people. Some computer users do not think sharing files matters, but many of the people who make the music and videos, and who own the copyright, say that file sharing is stealing.

Setbacks

It took Karlheinz Brandenburg many years to develop MP3 files. The mathematics and the computer programming involved were very complicated. In 1991, after four years of work, Brandenburg nearly gave up because of errors in the **software** that compressed and played the MP3 files.

Listening to music together is fun, but you must not make copies of music files.

25

2006—Sony releases its PlayStation 3 console

2010

INTO THE FUTURE

Modern computers, even everyday personal computers, are extraordinary machines. Inside them are **microprocessors** capable of doing millions of calculations every second. These amazingly complicated **microchips**, just a few centimeters across, contain hundreds of millions of tiny components. Also inside are **memory** chips that can remember billions of pieces of information. Computers can store our music, photographs, and videos. The **Internet** connects computers all over the planet, allowing us to keep in touch with other people, find almost any information on the World Wide Web, entertain ourselves with music and videos, and even go shopping. Imagine what Charles Babbage would think of modern computers, if he could see them today!

Computers are often used in classrooms. Children learn computer skills, as well as how to find and present information for all the other subjects they study.

Setbacks

Computers have a downside. Their main problem is their effect on the planet. Computers use electricity, and so they add to the carbon emissions that are driving **global warming**. Computers quickly become too old and slow to use the latest **software**, and disposing of all the old computers and printers is very bad for the environment. Many computers are used again or their parts and materials are recycled, but tens of millions are dumped into landfill sites every year.

Can you think of some good ways to reuse old computers and their parts?

Every few months, new, more powerful computers are introduced. Today, there are millions of different **application programs** that allow computers to do jobs from playing chess to designing gardens. What do you think computers will be able to do in the future?

TIMELINE

around 3000 BCE
The abacus is invented in Mesopotamia

around 200 BCE
The ancient Chinese begin using the abacus

1642 CE
Blaise Pascal invents a calculating machine

1943
The Colossus computer is complete

1941
Zuse completes his Z3 machine

1940
Turing builds the Bombe to decipher German codes

1944
Engineers at Harvard University and **IBM** build the Harvard Mark I

1945
Zuse's Z3 is destroyed in an air raid

1946
ENIAC is the first fully electronic computer

1975
Altair is the first personal computer

1972
The first home video-game console is introduced

1972
The computer game Pong is released

1975
Bill Gates and Paul Allen start a company called Microsoft

1978
The Space Invaders game is released

1981
Sinclair introduces the Timex Sinclair Spectrum 1000 home computer

2006
Sony releases its PlayStation 3 video-game console

2005
Microsoft releases its Xbox 360 video-game console

2004
Facebook social networking is launched

1801
Joseph Marie Jacquard invents the programmable loom

1823
Charles Babbage begins work on his Difference Engine

1833
Babbage begins work on the Analytical Engine

1938
Konrad Zuse builds the first **electromechanical** computer

1936
Alan Turing describes a modern-day computer

1846
Babbage tries to build Difference Engine No. 2

1947
Bell Laboratories announces the **transistor**

1958
The **integrated circuit** (**microchip**) is invented

1969
The first two computers on the **Internet** are linked

1972
Clive Sinclair sells the first pocket calculators

1971
Intel releases the Intel 4004 computer

1970
The computer mouse receives a **patent**

1981
IBM releases its IBM personal computer. **MS-DOS** is released on the IBM PC.

1985
First version of Microsoft Windows is released

1989
Tim Berners-Lee invents web browsing and the World Wide Web

2001
Apple introduces its first iPod

1998
The first MP3 players are released

1993
The **MP3 file** format is introduced

1991
The World Wide Web starts working

GLOSSARY

Allies group of countries including France, Great Britain, and the U.S. that joined together to fight in World Wars I and II

application program that makes a computer do a particular job, such as play a game or word processing

artificial intelligence branch of science that attempts to make computers react in an intelligent, "human" way

capacitor electronic component that stores electricity

current flow of electricity

D-Day name given to June 6, 1944, when, during World War II, Allies landed on the beaches of France

electromechanical uses electronic and mechanical parts

file collection of information stored on a computer, such as a music file, image file, or text file

global warming gradual increase in the temperature of Earth's atmosphere

hardware physical parts of a computer, such as the microprocessor, memory chips, and disc drives

IBM short for "International Business Machines," a large computer manufacturer

integrated circuit piece of semiconductor material with hundreds, thousands, or millions of components built on it to make a complex electronic circuit

Internet network that connects millions of computers all over the world

memory part of a computer where information is stored

microchip *see* integrated circuit

microprocessor "brain" of a computer that is controlled by a program, which moves and processes information

MP3 file computer file that contains all the information needed to play a piece of music

MS-DOS short for "Microsoft Disc Operating System," one of the first pieces of system software for personal computers

network two or more computers connected to each other so that they can share information

patent license from the government that gives a person or company the right to make and sell a product and to stop other companies from copying it

program list of instructions that controls what a computer does

resistor electronic component that slows down the flow of electricity

semiconductor material that can act as both a conductor (a material that allows electricity to flow through it) and an insulator (a material that prevents the flow of electricity)

software instructions and data that are stored in the computer's memory or on its discs. Software controls the hardware.

transistor electronic device that allows the strength of one electric current to control the strength of another electric current

vacuum tube finger-sized glass tube containing electronic components. They are also known as thermionic valves.

FIND OUT MORE

Book

Lemke, D. B. *Inventions and Discovery: Steve Jobs, Steven Wozniac, and the Personal Computer*. North Mankato, Minn.: Capstone, 2007.

Websites

This website has information about Konrad Zuse and his computers:
user.cs.tu-berlin.de/~zuse/Konrad_Zuse/index.html

Visit this website to find out more about the history of early computers:
www.computersciencelab.com/ComputerHistory/History.htm

This website has lots of information on the history of computers:
www.computerhistory.org

Find out the story of computer games at:
www.emuunlim.com/doteaters/play1sta1.htm

This website has information about the invention of the microchip:
www.ti.com/corp/docs/kilbyctr/jackbuilt.shtml

Places to visit

Computer History Museum
1401 N. Shoreline Boulevard
Mountain View, California 94043
www.computerhistory.org

Museum of Science
1 Science Park
Boston, Massachusetts 02114
www.mos.org

INDEX